Requiem for a Redbird

"What a joy to discover a young genius blooming in our hills here in West Virginia ... celebrating who he is and where he comes from. This is a wonderful book of poetry and I'm so glad to be one of the old women who can proudly say: Read This. It will make you proud."

— Nikki Giovanni, Poet

"A mountain mystic who is lyrical, chimerical, and gifted in both written and spoken word: Torli Bush is a species of poet you've never heard before. *Requiem for a Redbird* is one of the most original and honest explorations of race, class, spirit, and Appalachia I've read."

— Ann Pancake, Author of *Strange as This Weather Has Been*

©2024 Torli Bush

ISBN 979-8-9902208-1-2

Published by Pulley Press, an imprint of Clyde Hill Publishing

Cover and book design by Dan D Shafer

Requiem for a Redbird

TORLI BUSH

PULLEY PRESS

Table of Contents

I

- 7 — Ocean Spice Palace
- 8 — To Be Affrilachian
- 10 — The Death of Appalachia
- 12 — On WVU's "Academic Transformation"
- 14 — For the Collapsed Church on Route 15 between Diana and Flatwoods, West Virginia
- 15 — Behind My House in Parcoal, West Virginia, June 2019
- 17 — The closest thing to a miracle
- 18 — The Violinist
- 20 — For Keegan Lester
- 21 — In fellowship
- 22 — Riverside doxology
- 23 — Appalachian Bestiary
- 25 — Sago & Montcoal
- 27 — Haint
- 29 — Walking Along Little Elk Creek
- 30 — Another Basketball Poem
- 31 — Call the melody
- 32 — The Traveler
- 34 — 79/43
- 35 — 24th West State Street, Athens, Ohio
- 37 — At St. Stanislaus on 21st Street in Pittsburgh
- 38 — At the Black Sheep in Huntington
- 40 — The Shoats play at Gene's Beer Garden in Morgantown, West Virginia
- 41 — Tanka for the Old Bones in Webster Springs
- 42 — JD

II

47 Prayer on the loss of my Mother
50 Last night I dreamed I went to Parcoal again
52 Sestina for Jim
54 Elegy for Xanna
57 Master Electrician
58 Nightcrawler
60 Hymning on Willey Street
61 The Autumn Moon
62 Two Letters to Tom Andrews
64 Liturgical
65 The Field of Reeds
66 Sojourning
67 Liminal Redbird

III

71 Sequence of Accepting Your Body
72 Starlight Conflux
74 For the Fox Girl's Laugh
75 Walking along the Wolf Summit Trail
76 Your heart: a hitched metronome
77 Cooking During an Evening Storm
78 Dormant in Winter
79 At the Abbey on Butler Street in Pittsburgh
80 Hive minded
82 Ghosts haunt the Boiler Theatre
83 Driving Alone on Route 20 South at Night
84 The fox girl sits on a grave
85 Voltaic (adjective)
86 In your arms, I am home

IV

- 91   If my father's fear was confirmed
- 92   Visiting My Mother's Grave Alone for the First Time
- 94   Reflecting on a Dream in Which the First Boy Who Called Me Nigger Stabbed Me in My Right Lung Twice
- 95   Proper
- 96   Liberal Thug
- 99   Collective
- 102   QAnon
- 103   In which t'ai freedom ford, Terrance Hayes, Cameron Barnett, and Darth Maul emerge from my throat
- 104   Bones of Arlington
- 105   Blood
- 106   Ice
- 107   Mythoclast
- 108   Tanka for the marrow
- 109   Catechism

V

- 115   This Earthen Skin
- 116   WHEREAS Appalachia was always Black, queer, and wild
- 118   American Psalms
- 132   A Resolution on Christianity in the United States

- 137   Notes
- 143   Acknowledgements

For James, Frank, Xanna, Bernadette, Jimmy Lee, and Carol

Introduction

Torli Bush's *Requiem for a Redbird*, opens like a wide, bottomless seam of bituminous coal, filling number nine shovels full of truth and consequences. Before this collection even reaches its full stride and the tipple, we are chased off the basketball court by a thunderstorm, watching Mothman with a packed audience at a burlesque & drag show, and blessing the microphone with this poet at bars all over the mountains. This happens before our guide flies beyond Appalachia and takes all of America to task for her many, many sins.

Bush's debut collection is fire. The poems burn with a complicated love for, and criticism of, the region. The status quo shows up as

> "an atlas back to family
> cryptids
> blackness
> mine disasters
> God,"

rendering cinematic the glazed and often confused stares our speaker elicits simply because of the shrunken world views that have

> "never seen [or heard] black
> with a Webster County drawl
> southern pastor style,"

especially in the reclaimed spaces he helps convert from pizzas and pints into pulpits. This shapeshifting country preacher-engineer-Affrilachian poet-hyena-fisherman-Anansi tips his hat to the King James, but offers up an even newer testament, well-seasoned by the old.

These poems bear witness to a full-throttled life, challenged, and lived on the page at the intersection of everything that is family, identity, politics, faith, sex, and race. Separating himself from his peers and leaning comfortably into his space, Bush blazes a Black Appalachian Trail across every state road in and out of West "by God" Virginia, pilgrimaging from Huntington to Pittsburgh, returning home again and again to Parcoal like a homing pigeon to break bread, to lay to rest, to worship with all of those he acknowledges and claims as family. He extends his generosity and compassion so often and in so many directions that non-believers are welcome to the table without ever kneeling at an altar. These poems are not preachy. He is not proselytizing, though they do offer us some truth, and a way, and his life.

Requiem for a Redbird allows us to ride shotgun in an '03 Chevy Impala, bear witness to a grandmother's last breath, and co-sign the rebuking of J.D. Vance, while raising up Keegan Lester in his rightful place. The final poem in the collection, "A Resolution on Christianity in the United States," offers a benediction that is full of both the fire of a young Langston Hughes and the brimstone of James Baldwin; this piece puts Bush in conversation with all living poets speaking truth to power. Unfold your handkerchief, unwrap your hard candy, get comfortable in your pew, and get ready to pass the collection plate: Torli Bush is about to take you to church.

—Frank X Walker

I

Ocean spice palace:

land I have never known.
My mother, far from Grenada,
birthed me across the Gulf:
Biloxi boy shipwrecked
in Appalachia.

To be Affrilachian

is to be the coon
and the coon dog,
tree myself on the
highest branch to jump
noose tied, Judas:
guts bursting to make
love to the field
cause kissing my brother
is impossible.
I am both
not brown enough to be true
& just brown enough to be target,
and the white people I've
lived around my whole life
will ask why I put
my hands up,
take a knee,
can't breathe,
want to light
the stars
and bars on fire:
use the coal that killed my grandfather
and the sugar cane my mom's ancestors cut
to burn it like Sherman,
dust and ashes
consuming their "blood and soil."
The soil I grew up on
was West-by-God Virginia,
which is to say we have a
love affair with unions,
which is to say we know
how to teach old rich, white
bastards in suits a lesson.

To be Affrilachian
is to hold all of this
as a fire in my bosom
pen it down as a poem
under Holy Ghost inspiration;
call it a negro spiritual,
cause my soul is still south
of the Mason-Dixon
full of people whistling Dixie:
it is the old white man
with his four canine teeth
framing the black hole of his mouth
calling me *Nigger!*
on primary election day
in my hometown of Webster Springs
for holding a sign in protest:
We are all in God's image
and I stare into in his eyes
wanting to break all four frames
of that black hole
but I clutch the sign
bite my tongue
because my black mother, a poet, left her muse
to me as her dying gift after my birth,
and my white father, a sailor, taught me death
is the only thing to weep over:
her mother was a political revolutionary in Grenada,
his mother was a clerk and waitress in Webster Springs,
her father was a tailor in Barbados,
his father was a coal miner in Craigsville,
and I am an engineer in Bridgeport,
but that old stranger knew nothing of this.
Saw my skin and his eyes
went Fox News red as he said,
Fuck your Jesus.

The Death of Appalachia

Appalachia is a man tied face down
to the table of a grindstone.
Government, in his pressed pants
white shirt and red tie
has his Faded Glory dress shoe
to the heel of Appalachia's neck,
declares what Appalachia has told
his descendants for decades:
"Press your nose to it."
Capitalism, pressing the spin-pedal,
suddenly finds her skirt speckled scarlet.
Appalachia finds his nose gone,
the cavity riddled with blood;
Government keeps going,
teeth ripped out by the root
jaw unhinged, finally
bringing him up for a gasp of air.
This disheveled being only heaps
crimson fluid mingled with coal dust & steel shavings
on the marble bench
fo' he gives Capitalism and Government that look,
the look your pap gives you, fo' he tells
you to go pick your own switch.
The uppity pair
force his face back to the metal wheel
grinding his cheeks into a powder so fine
like that meth that keeps them crackers crazy
like that heroin that them redneck inbreds shoot up
like those opioids that turned the Huntington Fire Department
into the second coming of Jesus Christ.
Now, his eyes are torn out by the stalks,

crushed with a *schlick*
under the spin-pedal;
there is no dignity for him.
There never was dignity for him.

On WVU's "Academic Transformation"
(After Joseph Limer)

"Add to your faith, virtue
and to virtue, knowledge."
this scripture from 2 Peter
is the motto inlaid on the seal
of West Virginia University.

Its continuation, eventually,
brotherly kindness
but where is the kindness
in telling a brother his language
is not worthy of being taught?
In silencing a sister of her story,
written and on the stage?

In engineering, we learned the theoretical
is the groundwork for everything practical
and this is history practically repeating itself.

In Appalachia it is always a man
in a suit and tie burying us
under the mountains:
families, teachers, students
always cause they can't get enough
of that black rock,
always cause they can't get enough
money in their fists,
the same fists
they'd bloody your mouth with
for not kissing their dress shoes
while they robbed you
of an education, a future,

a livelihood, a way out,
a way back home.

Yet there has always been
hope in that bright blood red:
Sid Hatfield's red running down Matewan,
red kerchiefs running across Blair Mountain,
red shirts in the halls of the state Capitol,
the streets of Morgantown,
and the Red behind the words of Saint Peter
still etched in our seal as we look
to one another: "Add to your faith, virtue,
and to virtue, knowledge."

In September of 2023, WVU administration officials finalized their voting process to cut and restructure several academic programs which cut across all its colleges. The worst affected was the Eberly College of Arts and Sciences, which saw the erasure of nearly all its World Languages and the discontinuance of its graduate Mathematics program. Students spoke out publicly and to the Board of Governors against the changes; the overwhelming majority of university faculty also placed a vote of no confidence in university President E. Gordon Gee.

For the Collapsed Church on Route 15 between Diana and Flatwoods, West Virginia

I see the cobblestone cross in your yard
still whole, with JESUS etched into its center.
The black *Private Property* sign tacked on
your front by the threshold,
below where your rafters have
been spit from their ceiling:
jagged planks once crowned
by the smallest of steeples.
I imagine there were revivals in you once,
perhaps some souls awakened to Grace.
I imagine there was hypocrisy too,
I see it in others; I see it in myself,
like your eroding rot from being weather-beaten.
I wonder if you reflect *the Church* in America today.
We are a scattered fold,
we are wolves consuming sheep,
we are sheep cannibalizing each other.
This world is too loud,
but I see the cobblestone cross
in your front yard
with JESUS etched in its center;
I wonder who the Cornerstone will humble
and whom He will grind to powder.
I ponder if, in the end, I am like you:
a ruined temple with the Lord
left outside my front door.

Behind My House in Parcoal, West Virginia, June 2019

Still,
the Elk river is running
soft, verdant, constant
wearing away the stones
crying against the eternal smoothing.
Still,
my soul is a deer,
skittish, fleeting through the forest,
in a rut looking for love;
I'm told the last of these is a sin
before a ritual of courtship
and I wonder which hunter of men
will claim me at death: Yeshua or Satan.
Still,
The rain falls
and the sun scatters dual rainbows
trailing into these mountains;
I'm told the rainbow was a promise
to not flood the Earth, and rain is a mercy
given to the just and unjust
but the rivers consumed
Webster, Camden, Richwood,
and the whole south of West Virginia,
some three summers ago.
Still,
People are rebuilding
and there is a hope in that: to say,
"I still stand." like the rocks railing
against being worn.
I am told we humans are a stubborn sort.
Still,
Something, Someone
saw fit to make all of this:

a fever dream none of us could imagine.
I'm told that once a man & woman
were tempted by a serpent and
instead of leaving us, this Creator
broke into the fabric of everything:
a fountainhead of living water
smoothing out our calloused hearts
and I cannot help
but believe it
still.

The closest thing to a miracle

I remember is driving to your house in Cherry Falls
when my grandmother told me Shaina
was in surgery after her car accident.

I remember calling the pastor
who must've been busy at his day job
and your uncle, the assistant pastor,
who perhaps like the friend
of the man asking for bread
was asleep.

I showed up to your door with the bottle
of spearmint and eucalyptus oil as a backup:
my heart was burning to get to the church
because we don't speak in tongues but know that God
heals or at least abides with us in tragedy.

I remember us knocking on your uncle's door downtown,
heading to the empty sanctuary,
praying with that church oil dabbed on my forehead
your all's hands on my shoulders.

The surgeon's hands were steady,
her body and spirit fought to stay;
she healed quicker than expected.

Call it transfiguration,
Elijah visits the young woman
chariot descending
on a cloud of harvest rain.

The Violinist
(April 10, 2023)

The violinist in the Bridgeport Walmart parking lot
tells me he does not speak English,
his tan face carrying a mixture of joy and burden,
tells me his original language is Romanian.
For the first time I make actual use of Google Translate:

"I'm a poet and my mentor plays the violin
as a fiddle. I was curious if you were
interested in any shows."

                                          "I am not from here,
                                       I was in visiting family
                                          up in Harrisburg;
                                             I'm from St. Louis,
                                    ran into some problems
                                       traveling back home."

"How much do you need?"

                                                                "$500"

"I can't do all that but I can get you started."

If I was a fool let it be for the music's sake,
music that deserved to grace the Ruby Amphitheater
or 123 Pleasant Street in Morgantown
or the Lee Street Listening Room in Lewisburg
but was *here*.

A few vehicles pass,
one woman waves out the window:

"You play very well!"
The man takes it in stride
bowstring prayers continuing on the
sunny Easter Monday air.

For Keegan Lester,

I finally finished reading your book, *This shouldn't be beautiful but it was and it was all I had so I drew it*, from cover to cover: a moon dripping phases of itself in every line. To your waxing and waning continuously against a Manhattan sky. To your orbit being anchored in Appalachia. To your mind running faster than Pat White and bucking conventions like Owen Schmitt. To your grandmother stealing coal for her classmates. To science making you dream of the brontosaurus; to the people we've lost to science's drugs-for-profit scheme. To performing together in Philippi, Huntington, and Morgantown. To gathering the crowd close. To you reading on tabletops over mic stages. To Carnival in Brooklyn with my grandmother. To the Caribbean Islands' dancers in the street parade past Utica Avenue. To the food truck, and jerk chicken we had for lunch. To meeting your partner, Eleni. To St. John the Divine's Cathedral and its Poet's Corner. To you showing me a legacy. To reading you my poetry in Manhattan. To Mel's Burgers and that loaded mac & cheese burger. To every conversation on poetry reminding us the Muses said we belong here.

In fellowship,

I have taken
a liking to sourdough bread
savory,
toasted,
broken
with breakfast among the friends
around this table
as a simple way
to celebrate
our newness
after the pandemic winter.
It's our first Saturday
together,
in the new world
full of the vernal
storms that welcome
in the green,
the Earth's Deep Magic;
as such,
we have taken
the day to play
Dungeons & Dragons.

Riverside doxology
(For Marshall Hawkins)

after a new convert's baptism
reminds me of our nights
on Baker's Island
playing basketball til 1 AM

how I never could beat you
how you said you'd pick me
when you're a team captain
cause my defense is solid

your shot's just quicker
and it's just us tonight
and I could *feel* the air off the ball
just past my fingertips

head on a swivel to see the net swish
coleman lantern flickering
our dubstep/rock/rap mixtape
heaven's chorus

playing til our sweat was the Elk River
washing away what cancer took from us

Appalachian Bestiary

Mothman, Flatwoods Monster:
Silver Bridge collapse,
children lost to the night.
These old cryptids,
a superstition of real tragedy.

Don Blankenship:
29 lost in mine shaft explosion.
Gary Southern:
entire Kanawha Valley without clean water.

Men hearing their friends' blood wail
beneath a company's bottom line.
The Baldwin-Felts ghosts
are still wandering Blair mountain,
while the people hear the call of
redneck as insult.
As if fighting for money instead of scrip
was something to be ashamed of.

But Coal is the state religion,
and people ought to be
under the State's thumb, *right?*
Embrace poverty for our Savior,
cry its name in the streets,
until the air is blessed black,
and we forget every
miner's sacrifice.

I would rather be called heretic, apostate.
Be burned as a martyr
under the Rotunda declaring,

"Montani semper liberi!
Mountaineers are always free!"

My call
joining those old souls
still lost in the bedrock,
"Here world! Have your energy;
here world! Make your steel,
build your buildings.
Claim whatever you need
out of our old Appalachian bodies;
tear into our bones.
Coat our lungs in dust
as dark as the cosmos,
as dark as that damn,
God-forsaken gem
we give you everyday!"

Sago & Montcoal
(After the old time tune "Mannington No. 9")

Way out in Upshur
on Sago Road
there used to be a coal mine

On January 2, 2006
the lightning thought
it'd take a lick

For two long days
13 men in a safe room
beat the pipe
as a prayerful tune

MSHA pushed
as hard as they could
but in the end
only one stood

Young Randal McCloy
was 26
the other 12 buried
by the 10th

Brothers and fathers died
sons and cousins too
way down in that coal mine
mothers and daughters cried
the whole state mourned the news
men gone again before their time

Fast forward four years
April 2010
explosion heard
round every hollar and bend

At Upper Big Branch
we lost 29
said the mancar lines
were frayed like twine

MSHA said
it was the methane
Performance & Massey
couldn't contain

Weren't no justice
in the end
Blankenship just
had a year in the pen

Those numbers there
don't set right with me
29 men
worth 12.5 days a piece

Brothers and fathers died
sons and cousins too
way down in that coal mine
mothers and daughters cried
the whole state mourned the news
men gone again before their time

Men gone again before their time

Haint

I.
Those terrible eyes
holding a sickly amber glow
can be seen wandering the trees
every Thanksgiving.
All of Webster county takes the week off
to hunt bucks, and the older huntsmen follow
an unspoken honor:
Don't kill the does, they may birth in the spring.
Don't kill the fawns, there's not enough meat.
Don't kill the spikes, they're for the youth to take.

II.
His ghostly coat almost shimmers
beneath the stars and full harvest moon.
He cries no tears of blood for the fawns this year,
his nostrils smell no gunpowder in the dark,
only the ichor that filled his broken & rotting
tar black tines. Perhaps there would be no vengeance,
perhaps for a year he could rest.
He was an old thing, cast to earth by God
to the green of Appalachia where no one
ought to have lived
and the first people who did
left him well enough alone.

III.
His thought was short-lived as high beams
came into view a ways off:
foul stench and false thunder.
The death bleats of a doe,
his amber eyes now burning with scarlet and salt,

the smell of copper as he gores the poacher:
leaf-crunch snap of the man's bones
beneath his hooves,
made meal for the earth.

Walking Along Little Elk Creek
(After James Wright)

The sun glimmers the frost
of a hawk's corpse in a mown field,
viscera picked over by crows.

Across the river,
a train blows its warning trumpet
as it screeches onward to
the petroleum refinery.

I stop at the Dairy Mart
for a coffee, heavy on the cream.
Beside this store
two halves of a doublewide
stacked on each other
have been stripped of their siding,
the base wood rotted
from untold seasons
yet still together.

The road here
makes us
a house of cards.

Another Basketball Poem
(For Marshall Hawkins)

It was that time in middle school that the rain poured
back before Arden Cogar Sr.'s old pavilion
got torn down and they still held the springboard
event for Woodchopper's in the grass by
the basketball court and we still had the huge tree
for shade in between the two rims on the Elk River side.

It was just you and me that day and you were kicking my ass
on the court like usual, then the rain started pelting
like a sheet and we went under that grand old pavilion;
a flash and God clapped His hands in our ear,
a bolt between the triangle of trees on the center
of Baker's Island and we locked eyes
and made the call to run to your place on Golden Shore.

Crazy we were,
thinking that we could hop-step & dodge lightning,
that sheet of rain a baptism of adrenaline and fear
and we'd do it again, you know we'd do it again.

Call the melody

a kind of witchcraft or medicine work.
She'd tell you
they might be one and the same
as she plays lead and follow on her fiddle:
an old time tune to call you away
to the mountains or rivers
along the footpaths of muses or nymphs
but not sirens, never sirens
because the tune is always
the refrain of life.

A sound beyond
the church, porch, pavilion, stage
guiding you home to the almanac
your grandmother once swore
by in her youth,
the prayer your grandpa
would breathe past the fence on the wind
carried downstream on the Elk
for you to finish school and find good work,
the haunt of your mother's grave calling
you to live into the name she birthed you into.

You come back to yourself:
she is still trading lead and follow,
the notes woven into your heart.

The Traveler
(October 9, 2023)

At the Wal-Mart in Bridgeport,
fall has properly sat in
dawn and dusk flirting with frost;
midmorning, a woman stands
at the parking lot's edge
with a cardboard sign regarding rent.
She is looking to get to Weston,
half an hour south down I-79 by car.
I help how I can:
water, a spare change of gloves,
tell her Clarksburg might be easier
if the day draws on too long
and the cold sets back in.

As I leave, I remember the conversation
I overheard two richer couples having
at Julio's in Clarksburg not two weeks ago,
just as my partner and I finished our meal,
criticizing the Union Mission, the homeless,
the addicted.
One of the women,
I just want to know why can't they get a job?
and I wanted to turn and yell
What jobs?
One of the men goes on about
how one of his properties
would be worth more in Pittsburgh.
I see my partner's face turn scarlet,
her throat full of thunder held back.

I call for the check and we leave
knowing that dignity here
sometimes means
a still beating heart,
the crisp air in your lungs,
the willingness to ask for help.

79/43

There is always a bit of doubt
when I slot the key and turn it 90 degrees
from OFF to START.

She cranks, lets out a healthy roar of 6 cylinders;
I once heard that,
"Old GMs will run like shit longer than most cars'll run."
Giselle, my silver '03 Chevy Impala, is no exception.
My grandpa Jim picked her up with 11,000 miles,
now she's got over 250,
seen the states from San Diego to the Catskills.

She has this long-term relationship
with I-79 from Flatwoods to Pittsburgh
but we cheated on 79 a few times
with the 43 Turnpike:
all those service stations know how to treat
a well-worn car and a young man
who loves to make good time just right.
That's nothing to say of driving
under street and starlights between the mountains,
to and from,
the Steel City.

24th West State Street, Athens, Ohio
"The body is sacred, this space is sacred; this is all sacred, at least to me."
— Doug Van Gundy

An old concrete cornerstone amongst the bricks
of the Southeast Ohio History Center
reads, "First Christian Church" carved
in that particular style, you know the one,
between gothic and graveyard.

I didn't expect it to be the venue for
the burlesque and drag performance
of the Appalachian Studies Conference,
a juxtaposition of traditional and sensual:
organ pipes prominently above pulpit,
a small portion of stage extended out
as an open altar, contrasted with
showing face & skin to God to
music that definitely wasn't hymnals.
Although how long could you
take you & yours being made out
as demons by Fundamentalists calling
for your eradication from society?

Prior to the show, I met a woman
who was a mathematician looking to turn
writer, I'm an engineer in my day job,
so our conversation floated between genre
and differential equations, video games,
what we did to keep the numbers from
driving us mad.
A close friend of mine opened the show
as Mothman, dancing with wings
and being drawn to lamplight,

enjoying herself with the tease
and audience applause after.

I moved to leave as the third act of the list started,
when I got to the back, I stopped
briefly to say goodbye to Zach,
a cross-cultural activist
from the Cumberland Gap,
My eyes lingered on his gold cross necklace
with the etched sculpture of Christ.
"They don't make many with the INRI sign
at the top anymore." I said
"It was my grandma's." He said
I shook his hand, told him I'd be in touch.

Walking out, I looked towards the stage again.
An elegant blonde in a long purple dress waltzed
with wide fold hand fans that trailed indigo veils:
separation and proximity, elements of prayer,
reclaiming Eden.

At St. Stanislaus on 21st Street in Pittsburgh
(For Deanna Briody)

I am surrounded by the company
of stained-glass saints.
Deanna, a friend two years my elder
and a Master of Theology,
anointed her head from a cleansing
basin held by a porcelain angel.
I am still learning that sacraments
vary by denomination.

She is Episcopal,
I am Methodist,
this cathedral is Catholic,
and here we are confessing
our foul speech
and vices of choice:
we recite in Romans 7
of Paul admitting
his own hypocrisy,
in Romans 8:
"What shall separate us
from the love of Christ?"
He who took on the nexus of the
world's transgressions and cried
"Eloi, Eloi, Lama Sabachthani!"

I am learning the gravity of
His being forsaken on the cross.
I do not mean to preach.
I only mean to profess
that it is an oasis
to be vulnerable
with your faults,
to learn of something sacred.

At the Black Sheep in Huntington
(For Keegan Lester)

                  we were Travelin' Appalachians
                  getting ready to read poems
on the bar stage
                        between
            Kelsie Cannon rocking on her Stratocaster
                 against bad love
and Sophia Rehak's soft
acoustic serenade
of leaving a small town
to *live*
                  everything we've written
                  about Appalachia
                is an atlas back to
                    family
                    cryptids
                  blackness
              mine disasters
                    God
                              my name was called first
                          the crowd must've never seen
                                      black
                      with a Webster County drawl
                          southern pastor style
                            getting amen stares
but I never saw the like of you, Keegan
that liquid courage taking you
                    off-stage
onto the front row empty table
                onto walking the bar
your poems fireside chats
spells for the porch and swing
and that moment

shouldn't have been beautiful
but it was
and it was all you had
so you drew it

The Shoats play at Gene's Beer Garden in Morgantown, West Virginia
(August 26, 2023)

Standing room only to hear
the four young boars play
guitar, fiddle, drum, upright bass,
billow old-time into the mic.

The Cup Series is running
a night race at Daytona
on the muted TV behind the bar;
an older man, a few drafts in, tells me
he's wanting Kevin Harvick to win.

I could've toasted him to that,
wished him well getting home.
This is the most "hillbilly" night I've had
in my 28 years on God's green Earth:

NASCAR,
two brothers dueling on fiddles
backtracked by bass,
my girlfriend's high haunt vocals
calling coal miners outta the grave
like Lazarus.

The whole bar called for one more song
and they could've lead us all
right off the clifftop.

Tanka for the Old Bones in Webster Springs

Sycamore planted
by the Elk River: roots dug
into anthracite.
Now, ashen testament of
a people working to death.

JD,

In some ways, our stories are alike. I was also raised by my white grandparents in Webster Springs, West Virginia, from the time I was seven years old. I'm black. Before your mind trails off too far: dad's white, mom's black, she died in the after of childbirth, brain aneurysm from having sickle cell anemia. Dad was in the Navy at the time, going with his parents was eventually the best option. I had a good life, I can admit that. I had some kind of anomalous privilege of growing up well off cause James Lee Bush, Sr., my grandfather, worked and retired from coal mining. I wanted to believe that your book wasn't that bad, that it was a feel good story that got misconstrued; I'm sorry no editor checked your ego at the door. If you would've stuck to memoir, the worst would've been you outing your grandmother as crazy enough to cap a man with a six-shooter; even that would've been too much cause everybody who's anybody who's Appalachian knows you don't paint your grandmother like that, JD. Like "hillbilly" was the only word that could define her; like she wasn't a "homemaker," like my grandmother, keeping you fed and clothed and getting the sense of needing an education into you.

You couldn't even bring yourself to admit what good you had, how it advantaged you. *Even being black and out of place, I can see what I had.* I saw my classmates too. Here's some people I graduated with: Tyler Neal didn't come from much but started his own timbering business and has a family, doing well for himself. Cassandra Clevenger lost her mom as a young woman; she's a pharmacist now. Aerial Lake had her house burn down our senior year; she pushed and pushed and did her undergrad in three years and became a physical therapist. Cameron Clutter became a barber, and can play a mean electric guitar. Samuel Canfield, a biologist, trying to help the changing environment. There's so many others in my class who went into a trade or healthcare or just outright working, *we ain't fucking lazy.*

I was the only black kid in my grade for most of my time up until highschool but I know that I ain't the only black person in the whole of Appalachia; where were people like me in that white monolith you wrote, JD? Tucked behind your ranting & raving on "welfare queens?" You just gonna pretend like we don't exist? Like we're all just rustbelt ghosts and magnolia tree ornaments? You ain't been to the core of Appalachia where the wild magic is: the hollars know every skin tone, it's kinda Christian, kinda queer, kinda folk, kinda soul food and moonshine; it's perfect dirt, fishing, hunting, and playing basketball into the nighttime til we bond around bonfires. There's an empty wicker chair and a mason jar with your name on it; come find me, learn who *we* really are.

II.

Prayer on the Loss of my Mother
(In memory of Carol Magdelyn Bush)

Abba Father,
I know it has been some time
since we last spoke.
But I remembered the verse
on generational curse
and have to ask
if that is why,
unlike Job,
I look upon the maid
with lust
again and again
and again.

You see, like David,
 in sin did my mother conceive me
 but name me Torli,
"Gift of God,"
and "The wages of sin is death
but the gift of God is eternal life
through Jesus Christ our Lord."
So, I wonder if my birth
causing her death
makes her the embodiment
of Romans 3:23?
Makes me declaration of faith
as she received the promise
and the brain aneurysm
was just her memories
going with her?

At this point,
ought I to cover my mouth
because I will surely be like
Job?
You will come to answer me
and I cannot look upon You
lest I be blasted Holy,
have to give up the ghost.
Maybe that is what I want;
there are 28 years to make up for,
and I just wanna see
both my grandfathers
dapping each other up
on a golden street,
but there are too many people
to worry about
on this side of death.

That would be Your answer.
That You orchestrated all of this,
from the cosmos to my life,
out of chaos;
what is chaos
if not a precursor to order?
What are You, my God,
if not spectacular?
At this point,
ought I to find
comfort in Holy Scripture,
in the still fresh blood
of Your Son on
the Dogwood tree,
that I am loved
by the Prince of the Universe

and the most beautiful
and precious of your daughters?

God, would you have me now
repent in dust and ashes,
press the coal to my lips like Isaiah?
This word is a fire
shut up in my bones
and I am weary with forbearance
and I cannot stay,
like Jeremiah,
these Lamentations of ink stains
are my sole connection
to the woman who birthed me.

Oh, how she must circle Your throne in praise!
How I must rejoice
in Your giving her leave
to visit my poems.
Lord, at this point
I ought to just…
[The supplicant covers their own mouth]

Last night I dreamed I went to Parcoal again,

on a night of all nights
I can not get out of my head.

A tree spirit called my grandfather out of his bed
into the neighbor's yard.
Had this happened five years prior,
he would have had the good sense to ward it off,
continue to sleep,
and I would've seen him in the morning
when we got ready for church.

Now, it has been five years since
and I can see the nymph this time tonight:
I do not bear hug my grandfather
waiting for the ambulance to come
and I do not chase the nymph away
nor tell my grandfather to come back in the house.

For it is warm and the cusp of summer
and he only wants someone who can understand
that his mind is going and he is dying;
so I turn the porchlight on,
run back inside briefly for a deck of cards:
clean, flat black, and laminated
with the seal of West Virginia State University.

We play Blackjack
and teach the tree spirit to do so
though she never hits.

Later, there is no conversation with my brother
in the hospital foyer.

My grandfather slept after a couple hands
and the stroke never happened;
his hazel eyes never turned to glass
and he died in his sleep that next Friday
like before but at home this time,
at home.

Sestina for Jim
(In Memory of James Lee Bush, Sr)

On the last day
we could call good
before the storm
took your speech, your walk, your memory,
all we did was talk
on the way to Sutton Dam to fish.

Fish
are such patient creatures in the day.
They settle in crevasses to talk
before the worm or corn looks too good
snapping their short-term memory;
a bite, a hook frenzying their nerves into a storm.

It's funny, we never caught a thing before being driven out by the storm.
So they got the last laugh, the fish.
I haven't went since, it's our last nice memory;
the last day
we could call good,
and all we did was talk.

Grandpa, I am dying to talk
like we did on the way home from the storm
when your mind was still partially good,
beyond that of a fish;
before the day
you talked to the tree in the front yard as a woman from your memory.

I hold this memory
next to the day

we watched that NASCAR race in Montreal. You could only talk
about the road course being hard on the brakes; there was no storm,
a couple cautions made the pack of cars sway like fish,
but every wreck you can walk away from is good.

There is a promise I hope to make good:
I'll carry this memory
of you the next time I fish,
and talk
into the storm
like when I slayed bluegill with you at Big Ditch Lake; what a day.

And there is that day way off we'll call good,
meet again after the storm of this life is just a memory:
you and I will fish and talk on that crystal river.

Elegy for Xanna
(In memory of Xanna Jane Bush)

        I. September 10th, 2023 — CAMC Memorial Hospital, Charleston, WV

How big did you say your grandparents'
farm was?

                                       264.22 Acres
                       and the walking path home
                     ran where the Burnsville Dam
                                              crosses

        [Catholic mass playing in the background]

You been listening to services all day?

                                                                   Yes.

What did you grow up in?
It wasn't Catholic.

                    No, Methodist. We was raised Methodist.

[We hold hands awhile, she checks her iPad eventually, we share goodbyes]

        II. September 12th, 2023 — An Evening Phone Call

Hey, I was just calling to see how you were?

                                I'm okay son, I'm okay.
                                      I'll be alright.

Did you have anything for dinner?

                    No, no; they brought me something,
                    but I never ate it. It makes me sick.

Yeah, yeah I know.
Well I was just calling to check
on you, I'll be down to see you
tomorrow evening.

> *[We exchange "I love yous" & "Goodnights,"*
> *I wake up in the morning to a text from my aunt]*

III. September 13th, 2023 — CAMC Memorial Hospital, Charleston, WV

I leave for Charleston that morning and stop
just after the 35th Street Bridge to speak with
Daniel Canterbury, a homeless man in his 60s,
whom I'd met before; he has the same distinct scar
of open heart surgery like my grandma.
I take him a couple more bottles of water,
tell him about my grandma not doing well.
He says he prays a lot, that he'd be praying for her.
We exchange a blessing goodbye
and I drive up the block to the hospital.

I got to the CPICU and said "Room 23" and the receptionist
let me go on without a badge. My grandma was still there
in that she was still alive and they tried to keep her comfortable;
I watch them unplug everything but the monitor
my aunts tell me she did everything she could to hold on this long
and I realize that my father is not going to make it in time
and I break, and my grandmother hears me break,
and I sit beside her resting my hand over hers then simply
over her arm as she clutched her chest to breathe
singular tear streak from her right eye
and in the middle of this blur she lets out an exasperated
"Yeah" to the ether.

And I wanted to give her the regards of everyone
who prayed for her, asked about her;
I wanted to read her Psalm 91 from my phone
because it was the one scripture she took comfort in
when my dad was on deployment, but I cannot start
and slip the phone back in my pocket.

I could only be there, only say "I love you"
only see the woman who raised me
fight past every remaining bit of her heart
that the doctors said declined from 15 percent
to 10 percent to this moment: the last beat
recorded on a scroll for us as her spirit left,
redbird free from her sparing cage.

Master Electrician,
(In memory of Jerry Bush)

man who could ride lightning.
Sportsman,
I remember you always outfishing
me and Jim
how any time we went to Sutton or Burnsville
you had to stop at McDonald's on the way home:
the chicken nuggets hit different at 11 PM.

I remember you and grandpa
having those matching '01 Dodge Intrepids
yours burgundy, his white
the two of you
making use of his garage
with the yellow toolbox
I've inherited:
full of sockets and wrenches
and dust and oil and grease
and now, our fingerprints.
I had the box out working
on the wiper blades of that Chevy Impala,
when grandma got a hold of me
that you passed.

I can only see Jim handing you your Ugly Stik,
the Lite model with the open face reel.
He probably had it sitting next to his Tiger-II
the whole time, wondering when you'd be around,
wondering if, for an eternity,
you could still catch fish out the mud.

Nightcrawler
(In Memory of Joseph Peter Limer)

A July night in East Liberty, Pittsburgh

I'm taking in that Presbyterian church again
                              the one across from the pizza joint
that has the steeple so tall you could sync
the whole district in your
                mind's eye
                leap
                of
                faith
                        into the body and blood
                              given for you
or any wine glass around
to take the edge off the sin and the pizza joint is also a bar
but also does poetry on Tuesday nights and I'm here again
                on stage
            Black Scarlet-Spider
            copy of a copy
              mask-on
          fighting to prove to myself
            this is where I belong
          weaving the web of my words
      so the place I'm from is never forgotten
          I swing back to my seat

and you Nightcrawler
flash onto the stage
pouring out your Filipino heritage like a
liturgy friars must've taught you
and there was a faith that stayed
after the rejection, and the humor in your

poetry was another flash step to defuse
feeling out of place til you worked up the idea
of us teaming up to save the Steel City.

Hymning on Willey Street
(In memory of Travis Stimeling)

Nine piece of fiddles,
guitars, and a mandolin,
narrows down,
the cat in the case
with the pig's foot,
and the catfish,
went still and our refrains collected
the West Virginia mine disaster
and bore it together through amazing grace
to where the soul of man never dies

The Autumn Moon
(After "The Winter Sun" by Mary Linscheid)

The autumn moon mirrors my soul
Of blessed feast and hollow
Of loved ones gone
Now safely home
The autumn moon mirrors my soul

Scarlet & gold plucked by the wind
Drifts upon the Elk again
Hark, hear the rush quickening
Gather now your harvest in

The fox rushes through the field
Coyote's chase never to yield
Bucks now clash their tines
And one's fate is sealed

Can you see the cardinal's flight
Your mother 'neath saffron light
The owl has gifted you its sight
On this holy All Saints night

The autumn moon mirrors my soul
Of blessed feast and hollow
Of loved ones gone
Now safely home
The autumn moon mirrors my soul

Two Letters to Tom Andrews

Tom,

I saw in the front page *Charleston Gazette*
where you were racing at Mt. Morris this weekend.
It has to be that engine sound right?
Nailing the turn to that cyclical hum.
I know the feeling but prefer *Gran Turismo*
to dirtbikes. It's always that game,
tenths of seconds to shave
at each corner, lost in that mechanical chorus:
brake, downshift, follow-through, ease the gas,
punch the gas. Pray that the gap behind you stays open,
that the one in front of you closes, your motor
the only one louder than your heartbeat,
the adrenaline a factor no doctor accounts for.

Tom,

The year just turned over.
I'm stuck in the four walls, in over

my head. Cause the pandemic ain't over
like your hemophilia was never over.

Now, I know why we push over
the limits of speed, over

distances our bodies shouldn't handle, over
the horizon to meet the One who is over

it all, to tell us life is never over.
A refraining chorus: it's never over.

Tom Andrews was a poet from Kanawha County, WV, whose collection "The Hemophiliac's Motorcycle" won the Iowa Poetry Prize in 1993. It is a collection that captures gravity, faith, gratitude, and humor; in reading it, one will wonder what stories of their own they have to tell and how many ways they can tell it. Andrews passed away in 2001 at the age of 40.

Liturgical

I.
Tossed in this whirlwind
of Your presence, I must ask:
why was this body's
shape formed after my father,
yet given my mother's soul?

II.
Will You descend now,
remind me of Genesis?
I am a sinner,
I too now groan with the Earth:
burn out this strange touch of death.

III.
When I am before
Your throne at the Judgement Day
I will keep silence.
If I am a castaway,
You're justified regardless.

IV.
The black desert sand
of sin collides with midnight
sky of holiness:
the moons witness my rebirth,
rising from Your oasis.

V.
I am a swallow
falling skyward into Your
new infinity:
the astral seas of heaven,
starbursts proclaiming Your reign.

The Field of Reeds
The Field of Reeds is a part of the Egyptian afterlife thought to be akin to paradise; the speaker does not come to this realm by way of death but by dreaming.

I have startled the wheat field,
Stag flees: a lost feast.
Leopard jolts in adrenaline,
I am prey,
her breath sending me beyond.

Conscious again on
the ruins of a stone bridge,
Ra flies westward over me.
Leopard mocks I cannot escape,
crushed beneath her heel again.

By moonlit river
she snarls, "You are not a man!"
Prancing circles she
goads me, "rear your fangs!"
Bastet plucks me skyward from the reeds.

I am given to Anansi
weaving star webs,
gifted silken light:
tether tracing the way back home,
a myth for my descendants.

I have startled the wheat field.
Stag and Leopard lay
upon the amber sheaves.
Her mouth crimson, in his flesh,
his eyes so strangely my own.

Sojourning

The sextant marks your
course among the stars, masthead
unfurled, siren song
laced on the ocean's salt breeze;
draw your sword.
Know you are not bound
to your own damned nadir.

Liminal Redbird

I know not which loved one
sent you as you flit past
the cinder stone path I walk;
I only pray the wind takes you,
as the Holy Spirit took them,
to a new, more joyous realm.

III.

Sequence of Accepting Your Body

I.
You carry the tones of your mother,
though it's shades lighter because of your father,
it marks every part of you;
your comingled skin is a blessing.
You aren't taboo.
You aren't fetish.
You share your mother's eyes,
coffee dark even in the brilliance of the sun;
she wanted you to see the truth of every life
being fashioned and kept in the Lord's hands.

II.
You don't know why the Lord took
your mother so young, in the after of your birth.
You don't know why the Lord fashioned
you as a man after your father.
You would that He'd made you
wholly after your mother instead.
You've found the expectations of a man
don't befit you.

III.
Your feminine is your wellspring of creation
because your mother's family
has birthed hope from plantation,
revolution from corruption,
and poetry from breath
as your mother did in carrying you.
You didn't ask for the responsibility
of a seed bearer,
but isn't the Lord wise?
Has He not given you a tender hand
to plant, water, and harvest
the fruits you are destined to yield?

Starlight Conflux
(After Paul Corman-Roberts & Allen Ginsberg)

Let's call it a cosmic Derecho
        stellar burst & implosion
                daisy chain ad infinitum
gravity drawing all the primordial soup
      back to singularity while we edge
each other at the edge
           of the milky way
                  anointed with the ice trails of passing comets
because there was nothing left
          for mankind to fuck away
                    and we left that pale blue dot
while everyone was fucking themselves
            or their friends or their friends' wives or
the forests or the mountains or the oceans
            or it was one man deciding to fuck over
a whole other country or the old fossilized
                fucks fucking the whole thing for their kids' kids
but you and I left well before that
            to howl into a void
                you wanted to birth a star from my seed
because Andromeda was so far away
          and Polaris said fuck us said we don't deserve
guidance or freedom anymore
          and faded to nothing
but you were determined to offset everything
                your creation engine a deep blood magic
that God made and found beautiful enough
              to come through Himself and you knew
that if someone else birthed God surely
        you could birth a star massive enough
                  to nova the singularity conflux

you knew beyond any doubts you were about
                      to set in motion the next iteration of the universe
I just so happened to be the raw material
                                  you wanted to start with

For the Fox Girl's Laugh

The hemlock forest with its nettled path
and pouring rain stifled
by a thick canopy forms
a tree leaf baptismal,
sprinkled on us.

The fox girl laughs at this confirmation;
feet wet with creek silt, hands pricked
with brush thorns: she points out
the Trinity's flower; Their hands
are still in everything.

I follow, hyena that I am,
relishing the cool of the stream,
feasting, growing fat
on her freshly dead tales
and the gristle of time.

Walking along the Wolf Summit Trail

we find the forest is a hallway of omens,
the twinned cycles of death and life:
a snapped bone, perhaps the femur of a deer
laying crossways in the path;
several shallow puddles home to dozens
of motile and wriggling tadpoles.

The midday spring sun will wring the water
skyward until these frogspawn
are dried, shriveled in the evening
like a fresh orchid's petals stripped
by a warm gust.

You notice every butterfly, transfixed
for a moment on the pairs of yellow wings
in flirtation but never coming together.
Oh, how our dance is like that!
And my heart is gliding,
a tiny emerald beetle flaring its wings.

Your heart: a hitched metronome,

2-3-3-2; fleeting starlight thoughts
of mischief or belonging
you'd never play out loud,
betrayed by a sonic almagest.

Cooking During an Evening Storm

Wind whistling,
thundercrash,
rain thrumming,
sharp scents of
crushed red pepper,
garlic,
sizzling venison,
a beep,
two clicks,
thundercrash,
time lapse,
rain thrumming,
aroma of fresh bread:
God's gift,
cork pop,
peaches & alcohol,
glasses clinking,
thundercrash,
rain thrumming,
savor salt, grease, fat,
fermented nectar,
fermented nectar from
another's lips,
rain thrumming,
thundercrash,
wind whistling.

Dormant in Winter

My soul is a moon
flower missing your halo
in the midnight sky.
Please, descend to perigee;
lift my face skyward with the wolves.

                                              Echoing howls
                            are the praise of your flourish
               here in my aura;
your dance mimics the tides,
rising from rest
to grace
me.

At the Abbey on Butler Street in Pittsburgh,

the hardwood decor balances between rustic and hipster.
I'm waiting on the lounge sofa outside the bar for you.

You show up with that black leather jacket,
the one with the faux fur hood trim
cause nights are cool here;
you've still got that short brunette hair all shine and waves.
I wanted to lean in and kiss you.
I love drinking with you
cause the confidence showed, I mean it showed before the scotch
but I loved the laugh behind the "fuck that"
to you not living your best life anymore while
I savored my rum & coke.

What would your best life have looked like right then?
I didn't care about the bar of patrons beside us,
just wanted to hear you muse.
I should've booked a penthouse room at the Courtyard
overlooking the Allegheny River on 10th Street;
it would've been perfect.
I didn't because you were still married then
and some things should stay sacred.

Maybe the night ended properly:
sharing a pizza from Pesaro's in your car.
Still, if you would have pulled your seat or got in the back
or straddled me on the passenger's side,
I'd have savored it like the rum
and had you smelling of sugar cane when you got home.

Hive minded,

the yellow jackets are carousing
in a syrupy orgy at the
bottom of a mason jar
emptied of its sweet orange moonshine
not half an hour ago.

A luna moth hovers around
the bonfire: priestess chanting
praises for the full moon
and constellations
that backlight our shindig.
Now, I'm making out with
this slender pixie brunette
hands working around me:
a black widow's web,
citrus-flavored venom
stinging between our lips.

A ripening of the moon,
I find mine between her hips
& dreamsicle sips sweet
beneath my palate.
She'll cocoon me here
under her sheets til my
blood stills into her favorite earthy red wine
or else til I sprout monarch's wings,
and come up for air with the sunrise
split through their translucent membrane:
a prism of gold & embers
engulfing the bedroom.

Outside, the yellow jackets
are asleep in the jar.
I tap the side with a tuning fork
and run for the back porch.

Ghosts haunt the Boiler Theatre

of Davis & Elkins College or so the fraternity
tales go. The fiddler gal told me it wasn't
quite like that:

They live in the walls, students leave a part of
themselves on the stage enough
it leaves an imprint. They don't come out
'cept when I play for 'em. Old time and Country,
something the mountains always echoed
in Elkins. And if you got any stones,
you'll come see it tonight.

She lead me through to an old rehearsal floor,
taken over by strewn stage lights
and carpentry equipment.
Unhooking her case, she drew her fiddle
and bow, playing a smooth dance number
as I sat in a corner windowsill.

I am a writer, no stranger to tricks of the eye,
spirits deciding they're your muse or
your Virgil: a guide pulling you forward.
But this was the reverse, every shade she
conjured sat, gave a piece of themselves:
a recital of each of their characters' gratitude.
Anansi lowered from the ceiling on a silk thread,
skittered into my palm:

Write this, I don't know what
other sign to give you. Write this.

Driving Alone on Route 20 South at Night,

lightning dances in the sky without
rhythmic rain, illuminating the mountains'
ridgelines. A tomboy who likes me
told me they love most storms
and we both enjoy watching arcs flash
and I'm thinking now about electricity
between bodies: nerves jolting
into a golden ionic trace on synapses
from hands tracing curves in a bare
moon-lit, calf-low river tryst, dancing
with fireflies flickering on the bank.
Orpheus plays on his lyre gazing
at Ursa Major on a celestial night walk,
and there is a joy so great that the
spirits & nymphs & demons & angels
& deities pause in their squabbles.
Calliope anoints my head,
Apollo rebirths my lover
into a daemon of all arts.
There is a consummance where I kneel
am baptized in river salt,
drowning with their tang on my lips
with tufts of my bangs being gripped
and pulled close.
Dionysus refills their chalice
as they howl
profane thunder at the moon.

The fox girl sits on a grave

in the old Oak Grove Cemetery
in Morgantown, beyond the witching hour.

Eyeing the constellations,
she beckons for me to follow,
traces Cassiopeia, Orion, Sagittarius awake,
no thought that the Queen may send
the Hunter and the Archer after us:
scavengers glutton upon moonlight.

Voltaic (adjective) —

The touch of my partner in a word:
a static discharge quickening
the embers within
the sensitive nerves of
my back, the crook of my neck,
a feather-finger tracing of
my collarbones.
My light-skin always forgets what
affection is;
my body curls like a feline
and the absence reminds me
why I crave it;
I know then that I am wanted
and present
and not forbidden
nor too dark
nor a fetish solely
for the *eyes* of white women.
Blush, my black joy,
staining my howl
moonbeam after the storm.

In your arms, I am home
(For Mary Linscheid)

my heart beats
faster than our orbit of the sun
and I can feel yours likewise
a harmonic roulette

beneath their cages of bone
with the syncopation of river & woods
singing for the ethereal oneness
only the archangels could know
the edenic goodness of birdsong

moonflower blossoms
unknowing & unashamed of our nakedness
in the long shadow of the autumnal foliage
the Appalachian nymphs anointing us
choosing to be our muses

giving our voices the gift of these mountains
to call up the dry bones of coal's ghost-king reign
reclaim every bastion from his wicked court
bring our stories, our music, our people
home

IV.

If my father's fear was confirmed

and my mother's grave was desecrated
for being a black woman
buried in Heaters, West Virginia
amidst the Brown and Bush families
from Burnsville and Webster Springs
her spirit would not haunt the exhumists.
She would gather her bones working the winds into gusts
with her hands and push them south
beyond the Caribbean Sea to the Grenadian sands
where her father's ashes are now scattered.
She would walk to Biloxi, Mississippi to gather the bushel of roses
from my father that never made it to the delivery room,
linger in that delivery room until she could forgive
the new doctor who waited too late to give her the epidural,
until she could remember the joy of being so great with child.
She would leave the room to go see the child, a son,
now grown, his life confirming her joy.
Then she would go to the rest of her loved ones
taking in the resolve of her mother,
the success of her husband, now remarried,
but seeing the ghosts of his grief for her.
She would not haunt the exhumists;
She would walk the Caribbean Sea
to the arms of her father,
to the scents of spice
from a forgotten lifetime.

Visiting My Mother's Grave Alone for the First Time
(Little Kanawha Memorial Gardens, Heaters, WV— May 25, 2020)

I am feeling beautiful as your son
for the first time;
I am sorry that I have put off
embracing how much of your
nature you left with me.

I wish I could have known you,
yet there will be an eternity for that
later in Heaven;
what longing I have to hug you
for the first time,
apologize for all the missteps
and any way I failed to live into your
expectations,
though everyone would tell me
you had none.

I wanna sing hymns and do poems
in the amphitheater of New Jerusalem
with you, ecstatic and unapologetic
praise to Adonai who saw fit
to have us first meet as perfected spirits;
I am trying to carry good hope this time.

There is enough grief;
the rest of the family says I remind
them of you though I still have
dad's voice.
I've tried to find what my own
being means:
a kaleidoscope of your grace
and dad's sense of justice.

I am feeling beautiful
for the first time as your son,
because I carry your love with me.

Reflecting on a Dream in Which the First Boy Who Called Me Nigger Stabbed Me in My Right Lung Twice

I don't know why dream deaths feel so tangible. I don't know why you appeared to me, Toby. We haven't spoken in years, and you are far from that blue-eyed, blond kid who called me outside my name. Maybe you were a symbol this time, but my sleep has no need to paint you as a villain, so what then? Forerunner, warning me that my home is no longer safe, or that it never truly was? I don't blame you for playing your part in this vision: Webster County was its own hell once for people of my skin. Perhaps that is why my grandmother told me I wasn't black when Marleena called me a nigger before you did, why others still tell me I'm more "culturally white" cause I'm mixed and grew up in-between three mountains not knowing if any trees were familiar with the grasp of a throat. Toby, if I see you in my dreams again, I hope we'll be playing football together like we did in grade school. Maybe, I can hit my blocks right and carve a path to daylight for you.

Proper

As in "You're so smart."

As in "Turn that rap off."

As in "You're light enough, my dad might just see you as you."

As in "I've always seen you as more culturally white."

As in "I never expected you to step out of line."

As in "Why do you speak so formally?"

As in "You're mixed, not black."

As in "We both think you'd be a good fuck."

Liberal Thug

"If a Black man [H.K. Edgerton] can't change ya trying to tell the truth about any of it [Confederate history] then you're about like the other liberal thugs."
— James Varney

To Hell with your seaport taxes,
Lee signed the surrender at Appomattox.

I guess I'm gonna have to go Willy T.
show up to your shop with some Willy Pete
make the fire streak
like I'm marching to the sea.

Thug? Who am I running with?
John Brown, rednecks in kerchiefs?
Abolition sometimes requires
demolition.

Got no love for your ancestors
in gray coats,
in Cocytus, frozen
sucking Davis's chode.

Stephens said the confederacy
was to keep the negro
under the boot of white supremacy;
how does that leather taste?

This is my grandad's .35 Marlin
aimed right at your face
talking bout how the Confederacy
might've made things more Godly.

Godly: keeping other people in chains
Godly: beating them til their blood became rain
Godly: hanging them from a tree
with everything but a crown of thorns
to declare their majesty.

To Hell with your seaport taxes,
Lee signed the surrender at Appomattox.

Your Dixieland only lasted four years
Its legacy Post-Reconstruction well into Jim Crow
was lynching and bombing and 2-inch hose
and hoes mad accusing, see Richard & Emmett

Burning Tulsa, flood in Money
Their depravity had no limits.
Where's the righteousness in it?

I can tell you what made HK Edgerton
coon coat, it was gray camo.
He probably saw negroes
getting J-F-KO'D, R-F-KO'D
figured he'd be another Medgar
Evers outside of his home.

Made your all's token in bad faith,
get outta my face.
Telling me you don't see color,
but still believe in marital segregation;
am I an abomination?

Whatcha got left for me Jim?
You wanted a liberal thug
you got him.
This writing came from

New Negro, Harlem Renaissance,
and Pittsburgh grit;
Wesleyan-bred Bobcat
meaning I don't quit.

It's Affrilachian contemporaries
with that rhythm & rhyme;
Appalachian mentors
on soul & old time.

The mountains in my voice,
Caribbean in my blood;
you left me no choice,
Imma show you what's good.

Imma bury you under
the yuccas
sucker; already told you twice
so you know what it is.

Already told you twice
but I'll tell you again.
To Hell with your seaport taxes,
Lee signed the surrender at Appomattox.

Collective

This rugged individualism is detrimental
This rugged individualism is detrimental
This rugged individualism is detrimental
We are freaking essential

Black Lives Matter on the mask upon my face
You say "all lives,", don't know how much grace
I can extend. Your ideologies put bodies in the grave
There's no end; everything's a conspiracy:

The nurses, the cold trucks, the morgues, the vaccines
Everything outside your white washed wet dream
Spiked rot in your lungs
Serpent's silver your tongue

I need a minute to breathe
I need a minute to grieve
A million plus dead bodies in the ground
I mean, sheesh

How you gonna call this mask a leash
then turn around
and preach
about horse dewormer, 5G, and bleach

This rugged individualism is detrimental
This rugged individualism is detrimental
This rugged individualism is detrimental
We are freaking essential

My patience has worn thin
"God's will, thoughts & prayers" close the casket again

but I know it's the devil
and he's wearing your grin

See the whites of my eyes
the exhaustion, tears I've cried
for lost loved ones, lost caution
for speaking out of turn

The virus just wanted to watch the world burn
Did you catch it? Did you bring it home?
Did you protect yourself and others
or were you "When in Rome…"?

Can you tell me what would break your heart
into flesh and crack the callous?
Would pall bearing finally snap the art
of your madness?

This rugged individualism is detrimental
This rugged individualism is detrimental
This rugged individualism is detrimental
We are freaking essential

Resilience
Humanity screaming against the pestilence
Insanity, politicians see me
sacrifice for economy

Tired of this cycle
Right versus rights
How can a man be civil
In the middle of this blight

Pleading again for normalcy
absent of your brutality

The sun also rises
call it justice, call it mercy

We're still here
Breathing steady
Fists lifted
Hearts ready

This rugged individualism is detrimental
This rugged individualism is detrimental
This rugged individualism is detrimental
We are freaking essential

QAnon

I'll have you know:

I want 5G nanotechnology in my blood
to chat with my friends telepathically
and stream hentai on demand.

I want to be an operator on the Jewish space laser
because burning Nazis never went out of fashion
and Epstein's Island should be an oceanic sinkhole.

I want serpent DNA so I can shapeshift and sense
the fear in your pheromones when I drag you
to the Illuminati for murdering your own children.

I want you to stop paralyzing yourself
with horse dewormer and get the vaccine
so you get horse testes instead:
the volume of ejaculate is guaranteed
to get your lover's approval
or disgust.

I want you to stop putting people
in hospitals, on ventilators.
They're rasping prayers to you:
a faceless idol.
I pray the space laser
fries your ass.

In which t'ai freedom ford, Terrance Hayes, Cameron Barnett, and Darth Maul emerge from my throat

You tell me that it is not too late
            for us to come together and correct our sins.
And in saying "our" you have lost me,
                but you say it is not too late…
                              Not too late for what?
The republic to fall?
It already has and you just can't see it;
          there is no law, no order, no justice.
                Justice is merely a construct of the current power base,
half of which is *frothing* to make my niggerskin
        the latest dance craze: the whip, the taser, the playdead,
            the torchlight T pose another lighting fixture
              in their churches where a "born again believer"
                  preaches our black lives are terrorism
                      while they praise a false god for a tangerine pig
leading his legion into the sea.
                So do not tell me it isn't too late
            when there is an assassin in blue
            and a cult in red hats
            resurrecting greycoat ghosts
                      attempting to burn this land
to the ground til it is nothing
              but white wood ash,
            and they will not stop
          until I and my kin are dying
for this maple skin we wear now.

This poem is composed primarily as a stitch of works from *& More Black* by t'ai freedom ford, *American Sonnets for My Past and Future Assassin* by Terrance Hayes, *The Drowning Boy's Guide to Water* by Cameron Barnett, and Darth Maul's monologue from *Phantom Apprentice*.

Bones of Arlington

Well there's a new religion in America today;
they worship a cloth god now.
When I pray to Christ
while its anthem plays they cry,
"Boy, why ain't you worshiping with us?!"
As if their flag was big enough to hold
all the bones of Arlington
when you fold it up,
could sop all the blood
of the dismembered bodies
of two World Wars, Korea,
Vietnam, Iraq, and Afghanistan.

Blood

Only used as a crutch when spilled,
never seen as an outcry
to be our kindred's keeper,
rage against shedding the sacred
instead of grafting our voice
onto the echo of fallen soldiers.

We call ourselves patriots
for championing a piece of fabric,
yet silencing the pleas
of their living brothers
hidden behind glassed eyes.
Shellshock confined to an acronym:

PTSD
and we speak in their place again,
vox contra fidelis.

Ice

Like the fear in her eyes,
                "Oh shit I shot him!"
Like Daunte Wright's blood
      still
drying
               on the concrete

        in the Minnesota chill.
Like Black
a thin sheet
              a collision
and every time
it's called
a fucking accident.

Mythoclast
(For Kyle Rittenhouse)

You'll be hailed hero,
right-wing savant, acquitted
atop two bodies:
brown folk now have answers to,
"What about white on white crime?"

Tanka for the marrow

cracked open, suckled
til the ivory hollows
clean, and is made stock:
Black alchemy of spices
makes the whole body a meal.

Catechism

I. Genesis

If a black man says he is in the image of God,
and a white man does not validate it;
is it still true?

II. Steepled Roof

If a black man under Christ's cross
is south of the Mason-Dixon,
will a white man under Dixie's cross
still make him a blood offering?

III. Ancestry

If a black man broke bread with you,
and told you every tale from
Anansi's tongue that survived
the Middle Passage until
the night cloaked you
both as kin,
is he still a savage?

IV. Sloth

If a black man had drugs
pushed into his community
by the government,
is he still looking for handouts?

V. Castile

If a black man complies
with a "blue" man's lawful orders
and is shot anyway,
is he still a thug?

VI. *Memphis*

If a white man tells a black man
to protest peacefully and another
white man assassinates him,
is it still gaslighting?

VII. *Compromise*

If the government tells a black man
he is no longer 3/5th of a person,
nor "separate but equal"
but fully integrated,
is he still a nigger?

VIII. *Parties*

If a black man is a Republican,
is he still a "coon";
if a black man is a Democrat
is he still a "sheep";
if a black man is Independent
is he still dangerous?

v.

This Earthen Skin
(After Langston Hughes)

This Earthen Skin
    is a gift
    is a rift
    between me and my kin,

This Earthen Skin
    is Anansi's spider silk weave
    is Adonai's stardust fallen through the sieve
    a story to tell when the night begins,

This Earthen Skin
    knows our mothers carry the weight of the sea
    knows they carry no higher glee
    than when our eyes first open,

This Earthen Skin
    breathes,
    bleeds
    the same shade of crimson,

This Earthen Skin
    pleads,
    "Please,
    I am not a sin."

WHEREAS Appalachia was always Black, queer,
and wild:

a sax solo following the guitar riffs of a grunge duo
rocking against *the man* at 123 Pleasant Street in Morgantown.

WHEREAS Pittsburgh is our Paris,
the Presbyterian church in East Liberty
a Notre Dame across from Capri's Pizzeria
where I started performing poetry.
The Abbey on Butler Street an apothecary,
an alternative healing through hospitality and wine.

WHEREAS the religiosity has a way of separating us,
I was the only Black person in my church growing up;
I say was cause I left it for Methodism,
not cause I left the faith altogether.
Many of us are still in the process of toppling White Jesus.

WHEREAS I have to get away from the fire & brimstone
so I run from Parcoal to Webster Springs and back every morning,
play basketball from 5PM to 1AM every weekend
for the entire summer with my rival of sixteen years
on the concrete courts of Baker's Island.

WHEREAS I return home to my grandmother's
corn-oil salt & peppered fried potatoes;
I throw some chicken in a skillet,
have a feast, and crash on the couch
cause my room's wall mounted AC
got infested with yellow jackets one summer
and my grandpa had to kill 'em and seal it up.

WHEREAS I'm having one of those wild dreams
of outrunning The Flatwoods Monster,
who swallows everything in his path
towards a pink sun horizon,
in my workhorse Chevy Impala
that my grandad got in 2005
when I was ten and hooked on the *Playstation 2*.

WHEREAS I stopped at a Tudor's
along the way, I figured I had the time.
It was only the end of the world.
Til I saw The Mothman chase his dinner
down with raspberry moonshine,
fly out the window at Mach 1,
and beat the Monster's green maw toothless
for threatening them biscuits.

WHEREAS I stepped through the exit of Tudor's
and found myself back in Pittsburgh
performing at City of Asylum: a haven
for writers escaping political persecution abroad;
what a hope to write in the face of injustice.

WHEREAS I remember going to Harper's Ferry
for the first time, learning about
Storer College and The Niagara Movement:
Black men becoming educators,
and planting seeds for the NAACP.
In West Virginia.

BE IT THEREFORE RESOLVED,
we have always been here:
the church,
the moonshine,
the wild music playing us out into the night.

American Psalms

I. *Of Blood and Flesh*

America is obsessed with consuming
black flesh and black blood:
an unholy covenant made with
the Dark Prince.
America thinks our blood tastes of rum,
he thinks our flesh Atlantic salt cured;
looks to set a fine meal before his queen, Babylon.

America told his servants to take and eat
and they did eat
and gained the Prince's silver tongue
and their tongues call us
thugs, animals, niggers,
anything to make us subhuman,
anything to make the blood sacrifice easier.

America tells our white brothers and sisters
of a God who will give them
power, wealth, their best life now.
They do not call that god by name.
They cannot, for he is not Adonai,
to Whom our spilled blood screams for Justice,
to Whom our burnt flesh is an incense of Wrath.

II. *Of Unity*

America,
I know that you would place
my head on a pike outside your gates.

I will be charged a critical race theorist
for being nothing more than black & poet:
lover of my kin's words.

Your apostates seek one religion
built upon our bones,
stained with our blood:

Ash of 16th St in Birmingham,
Memphis motel balcony ascension,
Emmanuel's prayer circle meeting gunfire.

When will you understand?
God cannot be wrung from our hands.

III. *Of Strange Fire*

America is burning every penny at the Dark Prince's altar.
A blasphemy of copper green flames swirl
as America presses his face to the marbled floor
of the National Cathedral whispering,

"Father below, have I not done everything you asked?
Was I not promised the world if I gave myself to you?"
America lifts his face and breathes in the solder smoke, a vision:

Columbia looks over her city and wails.
The dome of her capitol,
the columns of her congress and court
have all collapsed.
Her streets,
pregnant with the blood of immigrants,
burst open;
her people, choking on their own lungs,
leap from their rooftops to add their bodies to the red,
to pay tribute to her.
A streak of lightning sparks the viscera and corpses;
the stench of rot and copper perfume this offering:
The Dark Prince's gift to Columbia.
She never asked for this.

IV. *Of Inspiration*

Breath, given to us by YHWH
in the Genesis of creation
from formless oceanic void,
to the sun and moon,
to the skyline,
to the flora,
to the animals,
to us ... humans.
Clay and carbon and breath
skeletal sculpted, called good,
until the Fall; how did the knowledge
of good and evil lead to today?

Today, America, where my Black
brothers and sisters have their breath
stripped away by those sworn
to protect us, those who look upon
us with a fowler's eye and pistol,
I mean bow string, drawn.
Black bodies, like crows,
are a nuisance to those who
have serpents crawl out of their throats
to weave another temptation
that reality is a lie, "Trust justice, trust just us."

Is it any wonder our living kin
are turning the Dark Prince's strongholds,
like the Minneapolis 3rd Precinct,
into bonfires lighting a way
out of this tunnel vision nightmare?
A collective respiration after
choking in our own blood,
with a singular exhale: *"Enough."*

V. *Of Sadism*

How long America?
You have declared yourself a god
among the nations
yet look at your people.

See how the homeless are made criminal,
they have not tents, nor park bench,
nor sidewalk to rest their heads
for your magistrates have rent their tents
your carpenters and metal workers have
split the benches
your architects have erected spikes
upon the concrete.

See how the immigrant is met with hatred:
their children isolated, their women sterilized,
their men made into coyotes
running from coyotes while clutching rosaries;
was it because they did not worship you instead?

See how the people numb themselves
in the purposelessness you have left for them:
Black families in a constant mourning over
another loved one murdered,
another brother or sister sent
to your new plantation of prison.

See how you have raped the land of Appalachia,
the children have parents who OD to DOA
by the dozens because there ain't nothing
but nothing and poor is a news cycle
between Negro and Redneck
because not even your apotheosis
will save you from their combined rage.

VI. *Of Coal Dust*

America, do you even know
what a redneck is? Can you hear them?
The rasps of the [CONDEMNED]
beneath Blair and Upper Big Branch,
Will you pay what is owed?

bone
        upon
                bone
                          C
                          O
                          M
                          P
                          R
                          E
                          S
                          S
                          E
                          D
              into bituminous layers.
      The fiddle playing their funeral hymnals
          preaches this strange alchemy:
              blood makes electricity.

Will you pay what is owed?

VII. *Of Black Tar*

America, you have grown fat
breastfed on the deep,
coal black milk of oil fields.

Devourer, the sun swallowed by your
eagle, vomited from sky
flash fries city, desert becomes
glass.

Hell and
ire, both yours:
justification for creating
killing floors kicking dust-blood mist
long into the horizon of dunes kissing
moon rising into the starlight
nexus half a world away.

Omens walk the ceiling of your house,
praying that you choke on the deserted bones
quietly.
Rest beneath the Earth;
Sheol has found itself wanting for your
transgressions.

Under the sun all is
vanity and vexation of spirit!
Wise words of Solomon,
yet you wallow here an ignorant
zealot, ever latched to Babylon.

VIII. *Of Water*

How long America?
Your face turns back again
from the Mississippi Delta,
Biloxi and New Orleans
beset by water, bewitched
into hurricane curse by
the blood you've spilled.

Bones lifted
from flooded graves
and riverbeds say, *Witness.*

Obliterated wards
salted with glass finer than sand
say, *Witness.*

Tidal surge
volume of sorrow:
Witness.

IX. *Of Lamentation*

America, the man who your church
makes an idol calls immigrants *blood poison*:
a chorus of rabid cheers.

The Lord stands on Olivet
delivers beatitudes,
eyes towards the horizon.

At Patmos, He gives John visions:
Laodicea, last age
lukewarm, spewn forth to darkness.

Yet He stands here at your door
knocking, asking bread and drink,
offering His fellowship;

King of Kings, who still now calls humbly
to you, cast off with the least of His
for your hollow empire.

Their bone, blood, ash, dust, prayer
witness of our gluttony
upon them before the Lord.

He who says vengeance is His
shall have Michael pour us our due:
brimming chalice of wormwood.

What shall we answer this charge,
America? Let us choke,
Let the Adversary feast!

X. *Of Civility*

America, I can no longer in good conscience
approach your Republican *Party*
with a concept of civility.

There are still children in cages
at the southern border,
still families forever separated.

Their book banning & book burning has started.
They call teaching the history of people
who look like me Critical Race Theory.

White out Black, Red, Yellow, Brown
none of them are worth the dignity
of being in God's image.

A body is a body is a body to them
be they colored or white or victim or cop,
corpse on the red altar for the orange idol.

Insurrection has become acceptable to them.
I do not know what recourse there is
against these acts of fascism because

these people claim to do this
with God's blessing,
a heresy of the highest order.

They claim they are gods
to rule over the lives of others
and since they insist, I insist:

The *only* good Nazi is a dead one.
The only *good* Nazi is a dead one.
The only good Nazi is a *dead* one.

XI. *In Which the Capitol was Never Desecrated*

Harry Dunn and Eugene Goodman are not thin Black lines between liberty and death.

Michael Fanone does not plead with a mob to see his children again.

Jeffrey Smith and Howard Liebengood do not take their own lives.

Brian Sicknick does not lie in state.

William Evans returns home from his post.

XII. *In the Shadow of the Colossus*

In which Lady Liberty has
cast forth her crown
laid down her tome
took the torch and cried
for her sister, Justice.

In which Justice has heard Liberty,
removed her blindfold
seen the black, brown, yellow, and red bodies
killed, imprisoned, desecrated in her name
thrown her balance, now askew,
on the courthouse steps
taken up her sword and proclaimed,
Madness!

In which Goodness and Mercy
hear the shout of Justice and leave
David in the Valley of the Shadow
of Death with his sling and his faith,
come to our land and resurrect
the dishonored: a mass grave of dry bones
for the Lord to speak life into.

In which there is a quaking of Earth
and the blood of Oscar Martinez, his daughter,
those dead under ICE custody,
and the victims shot in El Paso
consume the Rio Grande;
the crimson flow, a wailing louder than Abel's.

In which all of their pleas,
from Liberty to the dead, are heard:
El Cristo Redentor descends

on His horse carrying
the sword of judgment in His voice
slaying the white-hooded
false prophet set in His place.

In which the Beatitudes are fulfilled,
and the mourning are comforted.

In which Justice fells her sword
upon the tyrants.

In which Goodness and Mercy
take the restored bones home.

In which Liberty calls all the
huddled masses into her arms.

A Resolution on Christianity in the United States

WHEREAS the Faith has been co-opted
by a political party for its expediency,

WHEREAS the Faith has been used
to the exclusion and exploitation
of vulnerable peoples,

WHEREAS sects of the Faith have sought
to suppress peoples in opposition
to state-sanctioned violence,

WHEREAS sects of the Faith have found
acceptable the use of violence
against elected federal representatives
of the public,

BE IT THEREFORE RESOLVED that we may hold
the following affirmations and denials
for the integrity of the Faith and separation
from the aforementioned practices
of the sects that have made shipwreck
of the Faith's witness in the public square:

I.

IN ACCORDANCE WITH John 3:16,
we affirm that salvation
is available to whoever would place faith
in Jesus Christ for the forgiveness of sins.

IN ACCORDANCE WITH Galatians 1:6–10,
we deny that this faith is contingent upon the support
of any political leader or ideology or that anything
apart from the Spirit is necessary as a mediator
between an individual and Christ.

II.

IN ACCORDANCE WITH Genesis 1:26–27,
we affirm that all people
are made in God's image
and have intrinsic worth
in their being as such.

IN ACCORDANCE WITH Matthew 5:38–48 and Matthew 22:34–40,
we deny any teaching that seeks
to participate in the harm of human beings
for they are immutably the image bearers of God.

III.

IN ACCORDANCE WITH Romans 12:1–13 and Galatians 3:28,
we affirm that the Faith
is comprised of many members
of diverse backgrounds and gifts.

IN ACCORDANCE WITH Acts 8:26–40 and Galatians 3:28,
we deny that anyone's race, sexuality, or gender
excludes them from fellowship with Christ and other Christians.

IV.

IN ACCORDANCE WITH James 1:27 and James 2:14–26,
we affirm that the Faith in Christ
which saves us
calls us to a transformed character and results
in works of service to others for their welfare and benefit.

IN ACCORDANCE WITH Romans 12:14–21,
we deny that the influence of the Faith
should be a cause of harm
or violence to others
or as a means to wield power over them.

V.

IN ACCORDANCE WITH Acts 1:1–11, 1 Thessalonians 4:13–18, and Revelation 21:1–22:21,
we affirm that Christ will return to fully redeem
what the Trinity created
in the New Heaven and New Earth.

IN ACCORDANCE WITH Revelation 21:1–22:21,
we deny that such redemption will occur
by any means apart from the return of Jesus Christ,
the only begotten of the Father,
born of the Virgin Mary,
given once for the sins of humanity,
risen upon the third day, ascended,
and now at the Father's right hand.
Amen.

Notes

1. *An American Psalm in the Shadow of the Colossus*: This poem first appeared in *100 Days in Appalachia*.

    "El Cristo Redentor"— Christ the Redeemer

2. *An American Psalm in Which the Capitol was Never Desecrated*: This poem first appeared in *100 Days in Appalachia*. The first four lines of this piece pertain to January 6th, but the fifth line about William Evans pertains to a later event in the spring when someone attempted to run a barricade at the Capitol with a vehicle.

3. *An American Psalm of Civility*: My viewpoint as expressed in this poem is against the structure of what the Republican Party has become and those who are actively working to change the framework of the government into something authoritarian and wholly other than the republic we have.

4. *An American Psalm of Coal Dust*: This poem first appeared in *100 Days in Appalachia*.

5. *An American Psalm of Strange Fire*: The use of "Columbia" here is as the female personification of the United States; she is depicted in ways that could be described as virtuous and honorific at times but colonizing at others.

6. *Behind My House in Parcoal, West Virginia, June 2019*: This poem previously appeared in the *Anthology of Appalachian Writers* — Ann Pancake Volume XVI.

7. *Blood*: "vox contra fidelis" — this line is roughly "voice against the faithful" and is meant to stand in contrast to the motto of the Marine Corps, "semper fidelis" or "always faithful." The poem is meant to stand as a critique with regard to the often shallow forms of patriotism this country presents while in reality such forms of patriotism are hollow or weaponized for political purposes of the sacrifices of the members of the armed forces.

8. *Collective:* This poem was originally written as an ekphrastic for WVU's *Healthcare is Human* photography collection.

9. *Hymning on Willey Street:* Each of the italics phrases are songs/fiddle tunes. *West Virginia Mine Disaster* is a ballad written by Jean Ritchie of Viper, Kentucky.

10. *If my father's fear was confirmed:* This poem first appeared in *K'in*. For important context, this poem came from a conversation with my uncle that he recalled having with my father shortly after my mother's death. Thankfully, she has rested peacefully and undisturbed but this poem was a way of reclaiming the very real fear that was present for my dad while honoring her and reconciling that she is buried far from her homeland of Grenada.

11. *JD:* This poem is an open letter to J.D. Vance that previously appeared in *100 Days in Appalachia*, *Black by God*, and the *Anthology of Appalachian Writers* — *Ann Pancake Volume XVI*. *Perfect Dirt* is a collection of essays by Keegan Lester that recounts his several experiences in West Virginia and elsewhere. It is far more real and representative of the people of Appalachia than the portrayal given by J.D. Vance in *Hillbilly Elegy*.

12. *Last night I dreamed I went to Parcoal again:* This poem first appeared in *K'in*.

13. *Liberal Thug:* This poem previously appeared in the *Anthology of Appalachian Writers Ann Pancake Volume XVI*.

"Cocytus" — The bottom layer of Hell in Dante's *Inferno*. Dante had presented the space as reserved for traitors such as Judas Iscariot and Lucifer.

"Richard & Emmett" — Dick Rowland and Emmett Till. Accusations against Dick Rowland lead to what would become the Tulsa Race Massacre; Emmett Till was lynched in Money, Mississippi, at the age of 14 and his killers disposed of his body in the Tallahatchie river.

14. *Nightcrawler:* Nightcrawler here refers to the X-Men hero. Joe had told me in a conversation that Nightcrawler was his favorite superhero because in spite of all that Nightcrawler faced, he maintained his Catholic faith and generally tried to be an encouragement to others. Joe was my first real mentor in writing and performing poetry, and he was emblematic of similar values in his own way.

15. *Ocean Spice Palace:* The title of this poem was inspired by Paul Corman-Roberts' collection *Bone Moon Palace*.

16. *Proper:* This poem was first published in *Callaloo*.

17. *Reflecting on a Dream in Which the First Boy Who Called Me Nigger Stabbed Me in My Right Lung Twice:* This poem was first published in *Callaloo*.

18. *Riverside doxology:* This poem first appeared in *100 Days in Appalachia*.

19. *Sago & Montcoal:* The tune "Mannington No. 9" was originally written by Keith McManus of Morgantown, West Virginia. My poem takes inspiration from the song as performed by Rachel Eddy at the Augusta Heritage Festival in Elkins, West Virginia.

20. *Tanka for the Old Bones in Webster Springs*: This poem previously appeared in the *Anthology of Appalachian Writers — Ann Pancake Volume XVI*.

21. *The Field of Reeds:* "The Stag" — The Stag is representative of the speaker's soul which the speaker is able to see in a type of out-of-body experience; in Egyptian mythology there is the concept of the *ba* in which a person's essence takes on an animal-like form. With the speaker's representation being a Stag, they are in need of freedom and forgiveness.

    "The Leopard" — The Leopard is a stalker and pursuer of the Stag and by extension the speaker. She is representative of guilt, shortcomings, and the adversarial nature the world imposes upon the soul. Just as the cycle of each day comes and goes so the Stag finds on some days he has escaped her and on other days, such as in the last stanza, that he has become her prey.

"Ra" — A prominent god in Egyptian mythology tied to the sun and the day/night cycle. His flight westward is meant to mark the sunsetting and transitioning to the moonlit scene of the next stanza.

"Bastet" — One of Ra's daughters associated with the arts, the moon, and thought of as a protective deity, hence her role in taking the speaker from danger and presenting the speaker to Anansi.

"Anansi" — While Anansi appears in this poem, he is not present in Egyptian mythology but is meant to act as a grounding for the speaker who has come into a foreign underworld. Anansi is of West African and Caribbean folklore, thus having ties to the speaker; he has close symbolisms with the spider and the role of a storyteller. The silk Anansi gives the speaker is to allow the speaker to eventually return home, awaken from his dream, and reflect upon it to pass the wisdom to his descendants.

22. *The Traveler:* This poem previously appeared in the *Anthology of Appalachian Writers—Ann Pancake Volume XVI*.

23. *To be Affrilachian:* This poem was first published in *Callaloo*.

24. *WHEREAS Appalachia was always black, queer, and wild:* This poem was first published in *Appalachian Lit*.

Acknowledgements

The journey to this collection was wild. I'm thankful to the Lord above and several people here that have given me the confidence and encouragement to press into this art. My journey into poetry was nothing short of a string of divinely drawn out coincidences. I'm beyond grateful to my family, all of the people in the following list, and many others I've crossed paths with along the way: Greta Dawson-Cox, Danny Ray Cutlip, Sarah Morton, Barrett Lipkin, Tatianna Evanisko, Mary Ann Samyn, Matt Gardner, Zach Cutler, Lauren Pizzurro, Lori Beth, Jason Burke, Sarah Rose, Deanna Briody, Davon Clark, Shane Manier, Brian Oliva, Elliott Carter, Kayla Lane-Obee, Larissa Evans, Claire Tryon, Howard Parsons, Brian Richards, Jen Iskow, Sophia Rehak, Kevin Chesser, The Travelin' Appalachians Revue, Brendan Rumney, Marshall Hawkins, Samuel Canfield, Amber King, Ian Lindskoog, Katy Ryan, Marc Harshman, Keegan Lester, Mary Linscheid, Frances McCue, and Pulley Press.

To Joe Limer, my first poetry mentor, for seeing a spark and cultivating it beyond just the competition of slam and into something impactful.

To Mary Carroll Hackett, Diane Gilliam, Doug Van Gundy, and my MFA cohorts at West Virginia Wesleyan College for honing my obsession to translate my voice to the page.

To Ann Pancake, for giving me a multitude of opportunities to rise to the occasion and present my poems to others.

To Frank X Walker and Nikki Giovanni, for their kind words and graciously trusting my work.

To James, Xanna, Frank, and Bernadette, my grandparents, for every lesson.

To Josh and Ryan, my brothers, that they know the world is theirs too.

To Jimmy Lee, my dad, for making everything work out in the end.

To Jocelyn, his wife, for keeping him grounded and showing me some of the beauty in Catholicism.

To Carol, my mother, for everything.

About the Author

Torli Bush is a poet from Webster Springs, WV. They hold a Bachelor's of Science in Mechanical Engineering from West Virginia University and a MFA in Creative Writing from West Virginia Wesleyan College. Torli is currently a poetry editor for *Heartwood* and their work has appeared in *K'in Literary Journal, Appalachian Lit, In the Shadow of the Mic: Three Decades of Slam Poetry in Pittsburgh*, and *Anthology of Appalachian Writers— Ann Pancake Volume XVI*. A significant portion of *Requiem for A Redbird*, originally entitled *American Psalms*, was also named as a Finalist for the 2023 Center for African American Poetry and Poetics Book Prize from the University of Pittsburgh.

www.ingramcontent.com/pod-product-compliance
Lightning Source LLC
Chambersburg PA
CBHW020201090426
42734CB00008B/905